LOVE IS ALWAYS LOSING AT
TENNIS

Written & Illustrated by
DON FERGUSON

PRICE/STERN/SLOAN
Publishers, Inc., Los Angeles
1983

For Evelyn

FOURTH PRINTING — AUGUST 1983

Copyright© 1976 by Don Ferguson
Published by Price/Stern/Sloan Publishers, Inc.
410 North La Cienega Boulevard, Los Angeles, California 90048

ISBN: 0-8431-0404-X

PREFACE

Although the game we know today as Tennis is one of Mankind's oldest, it didn't really become popular until 1223.

That was the year the Tennis Ball was invented.

Before that, the game consisted of going out in the backyard with a couple of Tennis Racquets and jumping up and down.

In Medieval English, this was called "playne tynnys," which meant going out in the backyard with a couple of Tennis Racquets and jumping up and down.

The invention of the Tennis Ball caused a revolution. And even though 436 Tennis Players were caught and hanged for their part in it, Tennis continued to catch on as a popular pastime.

By 1937, there were 3,000,000 Tennis Players in the U.S.A.

Last Sunday morning, there were 3,000,000 Tennis Players in Los Angeles' Griffith Park Public Courts men's room.

Why has Tennis become so popular in America? There are three main reasons:

(1) TENNIS IS CHEAPER THAN POLO BECAUSE YOU DON'T HAVE TO BUY A HORSE.

(2) EVERYONE KNOWS WHO BILLIE JEAN KING IS AND EVERYONE ADMIRES HIM VERY MUCH.

(3) A TENNIS COURT IS A GREAT PLACE TO GET SICK BECAUSE THERE ARE USUALLY MORE DOCTORS ON A TENNIS COURT THAN IN A HOSPITAL.

IMPORTANT TENNIS TERMS

FOREHAND: The part of the face above the eyebrows.

USLTA: Eskimo word for hitting snowballs with dead fish.

DROP SHOT: Doris Day's real name.

LINESMAN: Somebody who comes from the same home town in Europe you do.

OVERHEAD: Opposite of underhead.

CONTINENTAL GRIP: A virus disease. See Asian Flu.

RALLY: Sir Walter (1552-1618), Eng. courtier, navigator & hist.

CANNONBALL: A human being who eats human flesh.

LOBBING: The part of a theater where they sell popcorn.

TOURNAMENT: Apartment house with substandard sanitation, safety and comfort where poor people live.

DOUBLES: Playing Tennis with two fatheads — your partner and your partner's partner.

THE GRIP

Of the 1,769 ways to hold a Tennis Racquet, the most popular Grips are:

(1)   THE EASTERN

(2)   THE WESTERN

(3)   THE CONTINENTAL

There's no use wasting time explaining them.   None of them work.

There is no way a normal person can hold a Tennis Racquet and hit the Ball with it.

People who say they can are lying.

The BIENFANG GRIP (see Figure I) is just as useless as all the others, but at least you don't have to practice it. You simply pick up the Racquet and the hell with it.

FIGURE I

TENNIS BALLS

The first rule of Tennis is:

Always keep your eye on the Ball.

The second rule, particularly considering the type of people playing Tennis these days, is:

Keep an eye on your Racquet and any loose change you might have lying around.

There are two kinds of Tennis Balls:

    (1) EXPENSIVE ONES
    (2) CHEAP ONES

Always buy the cheap ones. Expensive Tennis Balls come in vacuum-sealed cans to keep them fresh and full of bounce. Cheap balls are about as bouncy as a pound of chopped liver. And anybody can hit a pound of chopped liver.

TENNIS SPORTSMANSHIP

Sportsmanship means playing fairly and courteously, with a graceful acceptance of the final score.

Sportsmanship plays an important role in Football, Basketball and Hockey. That's because the guys who play Football, Basketball and Hockey are 8 feet tall, weigh 300 pounds and will kill you if you try anything funny.

Since Tennis, on the other hand, is only played by ladies and sissies, Sportsmanship is unnecessary.

It's hard enough to hit the silly Ball without worrying about fair play and courtesy.

HOW TENNIS IS SCORED

Beginning Players are often baffled by Tennis scoring. Nothing seems to happen, yet the score keeps changing. Which is precisely the way Tennis is scored.

All you have to do is count how many times nothing happens.

Sometimes, but not always, when nothing happens, the score is 15. Or else it's 15-ALL. But now and then, it's 30-15.

In other words, when nothing happens, it counts for 15. Except when it's 40-30. Then it counts for 10. And then there's DEUCE. Nobody knows what that means!

In Tournaments, a Referee keeps score. This is considered to be one of the most hazardous jobs in sports. Each year, hundreds of Referees die of boredom.

TENNIS FASHION

Not long ago, silver lame' shorts, shocking pink sweaters and floppy hair ribbons were all the rage on the Tennis Courts of America. Today, however, most men wear white T-Shirts and double-knit shorts.

For the ladies, there's a wide range of Tennis Dresses. Your Tennis Instructor will be glad to assist you in the selection of a Tennis Dress.

Try to find one that doesn't pinch or grab. That goes for the Tennis Dress, too.

TENNIS COURTS

One of the fun things about Tennis these days is waiting for a Court, since it's practically impossible to get one. A good deal of money is won and lost on how many hours you'll have to wait. It can be days.

Why Tennis Courts are so popular is hard to understand. Most of them don't allow dancing or roller skating or even platform shoes. You can't do anything on a Tennis Court except bounce that Ball a-cross the Net.

You'd probably have a much better time in a bowling alley!

THE NET

The dictionary says a Net is a fabric wrought or woven into meshes. Actually, Net is one of the dumbest words in the dictionary.

Of much greater interest is Nestorian, the word that comes right before Net. A Nestorian is an adherent of Nestorius, Patriarch of Constantine, condemned as a heretic by the Council of Ephesus in 431.

The word after Net is Nether.

TENNIS STRATEGY

Tennis Strategy means taking advantage of your opponent's weaknesses.

An expert Strategist can reduce an opponent to a quivering mass of jelly before the first Ball is served.

Some extremely effective examples of Tennis Strategy are listed below:

(1) IF YOUR OPPONENT IS AN ALCOHOLIC, SHOW UP FOR THE GAME IN A BUDWEISER T-SHIRT.

(2) IF YOUR OPPONENT IS FOREIGN-BORN, INVITE YOUR LOCAL IMMIGRATION AUTHORITIES TO WATCH THE GAME.

(3) IF YOUR OPPONENT
HAS A HISTORY OF
MENTAL ILLNESS,
HAVE TWO GUYS IN
WHITE HOLD THE NET.

TENNIS RACQUETS

Some Tennis Racquets are strung with Nylon. Others are strung with (you should pardon the expression) sheep-gut.

Nylon is unaffected by weather and temperature. What happens to sheep-gut on a warm day would turn your stomach.

Aside from its more disgusting aspects, sheep-gut makes a pretty good Tennis Racquet, and most professionals use it. Look at it this way: If God didn't want Man to use sheep for Tennis Racquets, He wouldn't have given them such zingy guts.

STROKES

The three basic Strokes in Tennis are:

(1) THE FOREHAND

(2) THE BACKHAND

(3) THE SERVE

The Forehand is called "The Bread and Butter Stroke," but not very often, thank goodness.

The Forehand Stroke is illustrated above. Or below. Or someplace. It's very hard to get the words and pictures to come out right sometimes.

The Forehand is any swipe you make at a Tennis Ball on the right-hand side of your body. Unless your body is left-handed. Then it's just the opposite, probably.

THE BACKHAND

A Backhand is any shot you take at a Tennis Ball on the left-hand side of your body with your Racquet in your right hand unless you're left-handed.

As you can see from the above, the Backhand is hard to do, and damn hard to explain. And as you can see from the illustration, it's even harder to draw.

Most Tennis books tell you to use the Eastern Forehand Grip for the Backhand, with a quarter turn to the left and the thumb placed diagonally along the Racquet handle. If this doesn't make much sense, don't blame us. We copied it from another book.

TENNIS AS EXERCISE

Tennis isn't as much fun as push-ups, but it does keep you in better shape. Tennis is a "total fitness" activity. Five minutes of Tennis every day does more for your whole body than a glass of Tang and a Danish.

Medical experts will tell you that a slow pulse is a lot healthier than a fast pulse. A vigorous afternoon on the Courts will not only slow your pulse down, it may well stop it altogether.

A regular routine of exercises is essential to keeping fit. The exercise shown above is recommended for back injuries, if that's what you want.

CHOKING

Many players "choke" under the terrible tensions of Tennis.

"Choking" means tightening up and going to pieces, right in the middle of a game.

Even the best Players can "choke" and must often be removed from the Court, kicking and screaming.

The cause is usually psychological: an unresolved childhood conflict, or a deeply- rooted Oedipal anxiety has definitely been found to cause choking. A badly-anchored Jock Strap will do it, too.

PRO TENNIS

If you win five Tennis Tournaments a year, you can take home half a million dollars! And you don't even have to quit your job to win five Tournaments a year!

Rod Laver, an Australian, made $292,717 in 1971. And if a nobody from a foreign country who can't even speak English can do it, there's no reason why you can't.

LEARNING TO SERVE

A smashing Serve doesn't happen overnight. It takes years of practice.

Most beginners have a lot of trouble learning to Serve. They keep forgetting what wine goes with meat and what wine goes with fish, and whether you Serve from the right or the left.

But even though Serving is a fascinating subject, it really doesn't have anything to do with Tennis.

The Great Tennis Explosion occurred on February 16, 1967, in Waltham, Massachusetts. Eighteen people had their eyebrows blown off, and more than four other people hiccupped uncontrollably for three weeks as a result of the tragedy.

TENNIS MAGAZINES

To help you keep up with the rapidly changing world of Tennis, a large number of highly informative Tennis Magazines are available at your favorite newsstand.

These fine publications are chock full of helpful "how to" articles and important Tennis news.

Last month's "Tennis World," for example, had a stunning feature about how to repair your own Tennis shoes, an in-depth profile on the grass at Forest Hills, and 467 pictures of people hitting Tennis Balls.

TENNIS INSTRUCTION

Tennis isn't for everyone.

You must have the right personality.

You've got to be overpoweringly aggressive, murderously domineering, fiercely competitive, obsessively energetic, and well-liked by others.

But, most important, you really must enjoy playing. Most Beginners spend a lot of time and money before they really know if they like the game or not.

A much more sensible approach is to find out if you like Tennis before you go to all the ridiculous trouble of learning to play it.

Just about the best way to do this is to become a Tennis Instructor. There are a number of advantages to teaching Tennis before you know how to play it:

(1) THE PAY IS GOOD. TENNIS INSTRUCTORS GET ANYWHERE FROM $5 TO $25 FOR A HALF-HOUR LESSON.

(2) IT DOESN'T MAKE ANY DIFFERENCE WHAT YOU TELL YOUR STUDENTS BECAUSE THEY DON'T KNOW ANY MORE ABOUT TENNIS THAN YOU DO.

(3) TENNIS INSTRUCTORS CAN WATCH THEIR STUDENTS AND MAYBE FIGURE OUT HOW TO HOLD A TENNIS RACQUET.

For the lady Tennis Player in search of romance, Public Courts abound in opportunities.

GREAT NAMES IN TENNIS

Major Clopton Wingnut (1852-1927): Inventor of Table Tennis.

GREAT NAMES IN TENNIS

Carlotta Wills Zorg (1888-1943): Successfully overcame a childhood hormone imbalance to achieve fame as the "Father of American Tennis."

TENNIS ELBOW

No joint so captures the imagination as does the human Elbow.

Centuries ago, primitive man worshipped the Elbow as the center of the soul. He honestly believed that when he died, his Elbow flew out of his body and into a sea bird. It is from this primitive belief that we get the expression "What's a crummy joint like that doing in a nice gull like you?"

In spite of what most people think, Tennis Elbow has nothing to do with Tennis. The term seems to have been derived from "Tenochtitlan," the Aztec capital destroyed by the Spaniards in 1521.

Not surprisingly, the Aztecs responded to this by kicking the Spaniards in the Elbows. In time, anybody who had a sore Elbow was said to have a "Tenochtitlan Elbow" which eventually became

A Spaniard With
"Tenochtitlan
Elbow"

Tennis Elbow because nobody but an Aztec could say "Tenochtitlan."

There also seems to be some evidence that Tennis Elbow may be traceable to the popular indoor fertility ritual, "Tsimmis L'Bu," in which two teams of prebiblical Hebrews tried to toss an inflated virgin through an open-ended net suspended from a metal ring.

After the Armenian conquest of New Jersey in 1263 B.C., the Hebrews gave up this barbaric practice and opened a deli in Hackensack.

TYPES OF TENNIS PLAYERS

A recent study shows that people who play Tennis generally fall into one of three categories, and occasionally down elevator shafts. These three categories are:

(1) MEN

(2) WOMEN

(3) CHILDREN

To aid you in determining what category you are in, these categories are described below:

Category 3: These Tennis Players are usually smaller than category 1 and 2 Players. If you're less than 3 feet tall and weigh not more than 50 pounds, you're probably a category 3.

Category 2: These Players like to wear lipstick and funny dresses.

An extra picture of a Tennis Player that didn't seem to fit in anyplace else.

Category 1: These Players have hairy legs and smoke cigars.

Of course, these categories tend to overlap. If you're less than 3 feet tall, like to wear lipstick and have hairy legs, don't worry about your Tennis category. You've got enough to worry about already.

Proper off-the-court attire for gentlemen includes a pair of white ducks.

TM (TENNIS MEDITATION)

TM (Tennis Meditation) has been practised for centuries by Gurus who wanted to improve their Drop Shot. Confucius is said to have Tennis Meditated before he beat Kawasake Enduro 7-6, 3-6, 6-3 for the China Cup in 534 B.C.

Of all the consciousness-expanding meditation techniques, Tennis Meditation produces the most amazing results:

(1) TM (TENNIS MEDITA-TION) INCREASES THE BRAIN'S ALFALFA WAVE PRODUCTION AND HELPS FEED A STARVING WORLD.

(2) TM (TENNIS MEDITA-TION) IMPROVES YOUR SEX LIFE. TENNIS MEDITATORS NEVER JUMP OVER THE NET

AT THE END OF A
TENNIS GAME JUST TO
SHAKE HANDS.

(3) T M (T E N N I S
MEDITATION) PUTS
YOUR CONSCIOUSNESS
ON ANOTHER PLANE
(AFTER A HALF-HOUR
WAIT IN CHICAGO).

THE RULES OF TENNIS

All over the world, Tennis is played in strict accordance with the Official Code of The International Lawn Tennis Federation.

Beginning Tennis Players should memorize these Rules. Better yet, get a Lawyer to look them over for you. These rules are full of loopholes that can work to your advantage on the Tennis Court.

For example, the Rule Book says a Tennis Ball can't weigh less than 2-1/16 ounces.

Every time a new Ball is introduced in an important match, weigh it. You may not win the game, but you'll certainly drive your opponent crazy.

Here are a few more technicalities to raise:

(1) THE TWO POSTS THAT HOLD UP THE NET MUST BE 3'6" HIGH.

(2) THE SERVICE LINE MUST BE 21 FEET FROM THE NET.

(3) A TENNIS BALL MUST BOUNCE LESS THAN 58 INCHES AND MORE THAN 53 INCHES WHEN DROPPED FROM A HEIGHT OF 100 INCHES ON A CONCRETE FLOOR.

Another point: The Official Code of the International Lawn Tennis Federation doesn't say one word about Tennis Racquets. You can use anything you want to hit that silly Ball.

Tennis Player in the "Ready Position"

Tennis Player in the "Not Ready Position"

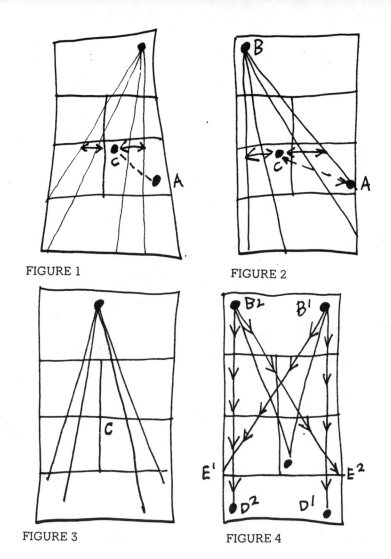

FIGURE 1

FIGURE 2

FIGURE 3

FIGURE 4

GAME DIAGRAMS

Study the figures on this page. (Or go out in the kitchen and make yourself a sandwich. It's your life!)

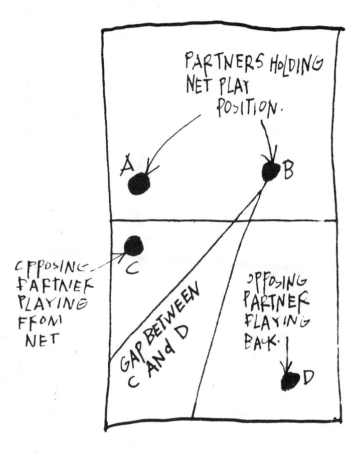

Look at the above Tennis diagram very carefully. How many mistakes can you find? (EXAMPLE: "B" is wearing only one shoe.)

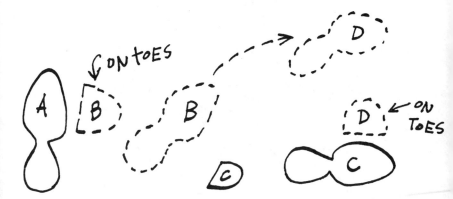

Footwork diagram showing how to walk like Groucho Marx.

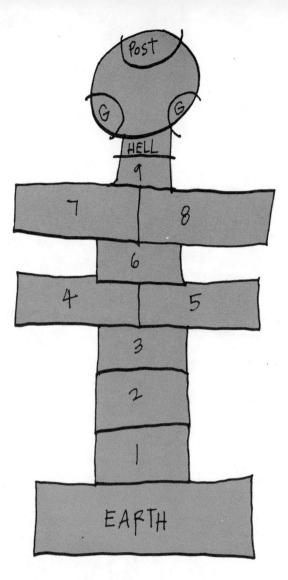

Game diagram of "Heaven and Earth Hopscotch" court. Note how totally different it is from a Tennis Court.

FIGURE MXVII: Among the Eskimos, a favorite weekend activity is hitting a snowball with a dead halibut. Although the sport has not caught on in America thus far, experts feel it's just a matter of time.

WARM-UP EXERCISES FOR TENNIS SPECTATORS

Next to getting zapped in the moosh by a Hockey puck, the most awful thing that can happen to a Sports Fan is "Tennis Neck."

Fortunately, only a few hundred Hockey fans get zapped by Hockey pucks each year.

But thousands of Tennis Fans go home from Tournaments with jammed necks.

Once it happens to you, there's not much you can do about it. (Your Doctor will tell you to go soak your head, but that's the way Doctors are.)

Illustration 46(a) shows an exercise you can do to strengthen your neck.

(1) STAND WITH YOUR FEET PLANTED FIRMLY ON THE FLOOR.

(2) SNAP YOUR HEAD AROUND AND LOOK OVER YOUR RIGHT SHOULDER.

(3) HOLD THIS POSITION FOR 30 SECONDS.

(4) NOW SNAP YOUR HEAD AROUND AND LOOK OVER YOUR LEFT SHOULDER.

(5) IF YOU'RE STILL LOOKING OVER YOUR RIGHT SHOULDER, DON'T SNAP SO HARD.

ILLUSTRATION 46(a): Neck strengthening exercise developed by noted neck expert and opera composer Giuseppe Vertebrae.

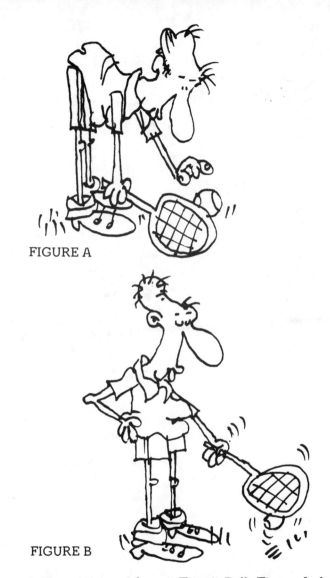

FIGURE A

FIGURE B

There are two ways to pick up a Tennis Ball. Figure A shows how sensible people pick up Tennis Balls. Figure B shows how Tennis Players do it.

TENNIS TIPS FROM THE CHAMPIONS

A demonstration of the Backhand by Evelyn Googlebong, three-time winner of the Goyisher Cup.

Tennis attire gives the wearer a clean-cut, wholesome, respectable look. Can you tell which of the two men pictured above is a prominent industrialist and which is a dangerous criminal?

If you said (A) is the prominent industrialist, you're wrong. (A) is out of work at the present time. (B) is a dealer in stolen Halvah.

This jaunty gingham-edged Tennis dress with matching bonnet is available in apricot, mint, lemon and pistachio. The Tennis Racquet is also available in 31 flavors.

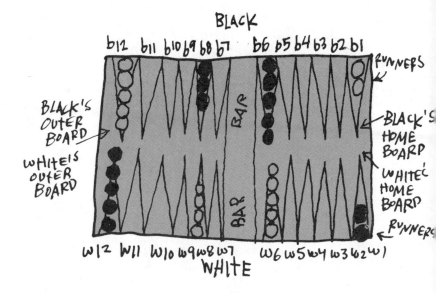

FIGURE 487: Diagram explaining Backgammon. Many Tennis Players play Tennis in the morning and Backgammon in the afternoon. The games are quite similar. They're both dumb.

ANSWERS TO THE 25 MOST FREQUENTLY ASKED TENNIS QUESTIONS

Beginners learn by asking questions. In Tennis, there are 25 questions that are asked over and over again. The answers to these 25 most frequently asked questions are listed below. Beginners will find it enormously helpful to memorize them:

(1) HELEN WILLS PIMBIK

(2) YES

(3) HAILE SELASSIE

(4) NO

(5) THEY ALL PLAYED CHARLIE CHAN

(6) WARREN HARDING

(7) CZECHOSLOVAKIA

(8) NEITHER

(9) TRUDI PRITZI

(10) 2.68 INCHES LONG

(11) HELLO

(12) "YOUR LIPS SAY NON NON, BUT THERE'S OUI OUI IN YOUR EYES"

(13) IT IS NATURE'S WAY OF PREVENTING EVERYTHING FROM HAPPENING AT ONCE

(14) ARTHUR ASHE AND LIONEL BARRYMORE

(15) ROD LAVER

(16) ARIADNE AUF NAXOS

(17) SANDY KOUFAX

(18) NO

(20) SHIRLEY TEMPLE'S GRANDFATHER

(21) WAVE THE FLAG FOR HUDSON HIGH, BOYS!

(22) HARVARD BUSINESS SCHOOL

(23) BOBBY HULL AND JULIE ANDREWS

(24) HONNI SOIT QUI MAL Y PENSE

(25) FOOTWORK

TEN MOST COMMON MISTAKES MADE BY BEGINNING TENNIS PLAYERS

The most common mistake made by Tennis Players is using plural verbs with singular nouns. The Tennis Player shown above should have said "The goods were ordered on Tuesday."

Beginning Tennis Players often make mistakes when they add up numbers. The Tennis Player in the picture above has forgotten to carry the one. The correct answer is 46.

Many Tennis Players think that "King Kong" was really a man in an ape suit. This is a common mistake made by Tennis Players. "King Kong" was an 18-inch animated model covered with rabbit fur.

One of the most irritating mistakes a Tennis Player can make is to completely ignore the F-sharp in the second bar of Wagner's "Das Rheingold" and whistle an ear-jarring F-natural instead.

Certainly one of the most frequently made mistakes among Tennis Players is thinking about buying a used VW without having a reputable mechanic look it over first.

Even championship Tennis Players frequently make the mistake of thinking Franchot Tone played "Captain McGregor" in the 1934 Paramount picture "The Lives of a Bengal Lancer" when, in fact, it was Gary Cooper.

The biggest mistake a young Tennis Player can make is to toss aside her dreams of finishing truck driving school and marry the first pretty face that comes along.